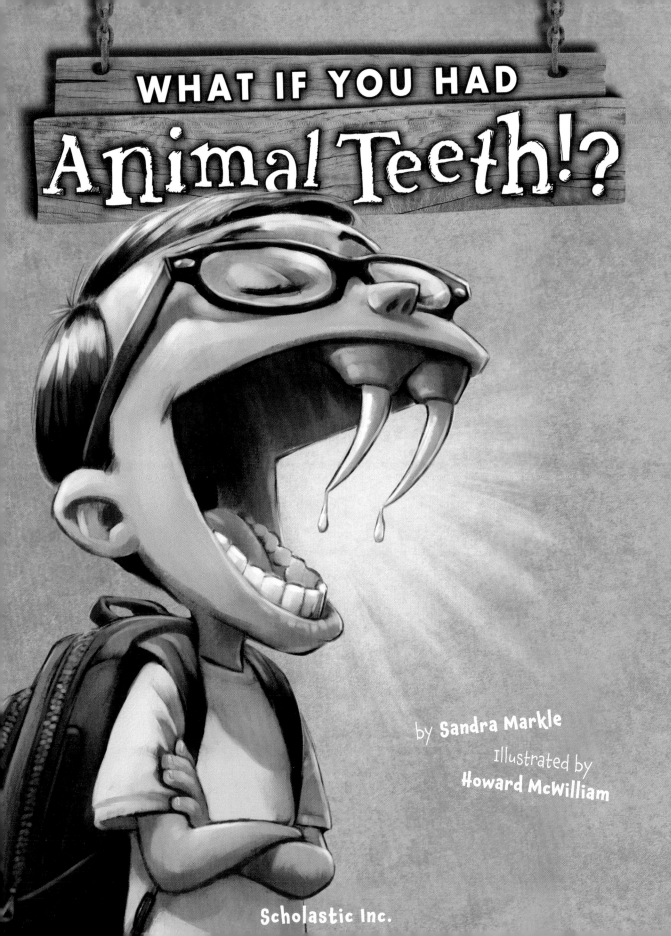

WHAT IF YOU HAD Animal Teeth!?

by Sandra Markle

Illustrated by Howard McWilliam

Scholastic Inc.

With love for
Allison and
Jacob Chase

Text copyright © 2013 by Sandra Markle
Illustrations copyright © 2013 by Howard McWilliam

All rights reserved. Published by Scholastic Inc., *Publishers since 1920.* SCHOLASTIC and associated logos are trademarks and/or registered trademarks of Scholastic Inc.

ISBN 978-0-545-48438-1

46 45 44 43 42 41   23/0

Printed in the U.S.A.   40
First printing, January 2013
Art direction by Paul W. Banks
Design by Kay Petronio

So you've lost your front teeth. Before you know it, two new ones will push right into their space. But what if an animal's teeth grew in, instead?

Beaver

A beaver's front teeth are shaped like chisels and are very sharp. They're perfect for biting off bark and cutting down trees.

FACT

A beaver's front teeth have a coating that contains iron. That makes them superstrong—and orange.

If you had beaver teeth, your front teeth would never stop growing. So you could gnaw all the tough stuff you like, day after day, for all of your life.

Great White Shark

A great white shark's front teeth are like all its others—two inches long with an edge like a steak knife. They're great for biting through superthick things, like an elephant seal's skin.

FACT

Great white sharks get new teeth about every one hundred days. That keeps their bite at its sharpest.

If you had great white shark teeth, you'd never have to worry about losing a tooth. There'd always be a new tooth growing behind it, ready to slide into place. And there'd never be a gap in your bite.

Narwhal

A narwhal's front teeth do something quite strange. The right one stays small, but the left one grows longer and longer and longer—to nearly ten feet. Once it's that big, it has a new name: Instead of a tooth, it's called a tusk.

FACT

A narwhal's long front tooth grows right through its upper lip.

What would you use your tusk for if you were a narwhal? Would you poke around to find fish or fight off your enemies? Or would you feel your way through the dark parts of the ocean? Even scientists wonder what a narwhal does with its tusk.

Elephant

An elephant's front teeth are called tusks, too. A male's tusks grow between five and seven inches longer each year of its life—the world-record elephant tusk was more than eleven feet long. They're great for digging water holes and pulling up tree roots to munch.

FACT

Elephants are right-tusked or left-tusked, meaning they use one tusk more than the other.

If you had elephant tusks as your front teeth, they would be superstrong, too. You could easily lift and move your bed or even the family car. And no one would bully you—not even tigers.

Rattlesnake

A rattlesnake's front teeth are called fangs. They're shaped like hooks and the tips are like needles. They fold up like a pocketknife when the snake closes its mouth, and snap forward when it opens wide.

FACT

When folded back, a rattlesnake's fangs slide inside fleshy covers. That way the needle tips don't nick the inside of the snake's mouth.

If you had rattlesnake fangs, your front teeth would inject deadly venom.
So your teeth would be all you'd need to fight enemies or to catch food to eat.

Naked Mole Rat

A naked mole rat's front teeth are shaped like shovels and are in front of its lips. They're perfect for digging the family's tunnels without getting a mouthful of dirt.

FACT

Like beavers, a naked mole rat's front teeth never stop growing. Biting hard roots and bulbs wears the teeth down so they don't get too long.

If you had naked mole rat front teeth, you could move each tooth, separately, to the left or the right. They'd work just like chopsticks for picking up food—bite by bite.

Vampire Bat

A vampire bat's front teeth are triangle-shaped and sharp as razors. They're perfect for scooping out a bit of an animal's skin so they can lap up the blood that flows into the wound.

FACT

Baby vampire bats have teeth. But for the first four months, they aren't strong enough to fly and hunt. So they nurse, and they eat vampire bat baby food, which is blood their mothers bring up from their stomachs.

If you had vampire bat front teeth, you wouldn't have to worry about them chipping. Since they'd lack a hard enamel coat, the edges would wear away easily and always stay sharp.

HiPPoPotamuS

A hippopotamus's front teeth are long, strong pegs with very sharp edges. They're powerful weapons, so opening wide to show them off helps hippos scare away their enemies, and the males to win a mate.

FACT

Because a hippo's teeth don't yellow over time, in the past, they were made into dentures. So some people used to eat with hippo teeth, including the first U.S. president, George Washington.

If you had hippopotamus front teeth, you'd never need to brush. Your upper teeth would grind against your lower ones, keeping them clean and white.

Bengal Tiger

A Bengal tiger's front teeth are a biting six-pack—four sharp pegs edged by twin pointed cones—set between its giant, daggerlike canines. They're perfect for scraping feathers off birds and meat off bones.

FACT

A mother tiger uses her front teeth to bite very gently as she picks up and moves her cubs.

If you had Bengal tiger front teeth, they'd be strongly anchored in your jaw. You could bite and hold tight while dragging something as heavy as five times your weight.

Crocodile

A crocodile's front teeth are all shaped like cones and have sharp tips. They bite well, but come out easily, and new ones grow in very slowly. So a crocodile's front teeth are always changing and are often different sizes.

FACT

Crocodiles can't clean their own teeth. They open their mouths for small birds, called plovers, to pick leftover food off their teeth.

If you had crocodile front teeth, your teeth would stick out when you closed your mouth. You wouldn't need to open wide when you went to the dentist or gave a toothy grin.

camel

A young camel's front teeth are long, strong, and have very sharp edges. They're just right for nipping off tough, thorny desert plants.

FACT

Baby camels' front teeth erupt through their gums by the time they're fourteen days old. Like you, camels have two sets of teeth. Camels get their adult front teeth when they're about five years old.

If you had camel front teeth and ate tough stuff eight hours a day, as camels do, by the time you were a grown-up, your front teeth would be no more than stubs.

Animal teeth could be cool for a while. But you don't use your front teeth to cut down trees or scare off enemies. You don't need them to dig tunnels, or

bite really tough stuff. And you never lift the family car with your teeth—
even for fun. So what kind of front teeth are right for you?

Luckily, you don't have to choose. The teeth that replace those you lost will be people teeth. They'll be what you need to bite apples, carrots, and corn on the cob; just what you need to help you talk; and, best of all, to show off when you smile.

Where Do Teeth Come From?

Adult teeth start growing inside your jawbone
soon after you're born—even while your baby teeth
are getting ready to push through your gums.

Any new, growing teeth are called tooth buds.

The crown, or top, of the tooth forms first.
Then the roots grow and push the tooth out.

When this happens with an adult tooth, it
makes the baby tooth's roots break down.

Next, the baby tooth gets loose and falls out.

Then the permanent adult tooth
moves into this space.

Teeth Need Care

Besides two front teeth, you'll get thirty more permanent teeth, but you only get one set, and they must last your whole life. So brush at least at both morning and night, and floss between teeth regularly. Avoid fizzy drinks and sugary foods. Those help bacteria grow. Then bacteria attacks teeth and causes tooth decay.

Dentists and doctors have found there is a strong connection between having healthy teeth and a healthy body. So taking good care of your teeth can help you grow up feeling like you have something to smile about. Plus, you'll have a beautiful smile that lasts a lifetime.